THE
TOWEL ORIGAMI

12 IRRESISTIBLE TOWEL CREATIONS

BOOK

THE
TOWEL ORIGAMI
12 IRRESISTIBLE TOWEL CREATIONS
BOOK

ALISON JENKINS

**Andrews McMeel
Publishing**

Kansas City

ANDREWS McMEEL PUBLISHING, LLC,
an Andrews McMeel Universal company,
4520 Main Street,
Kansas City, Missouri 64111.
www.andrewsmcmeel.com

ISBN-13: 978-0-7407-7126-2
ISBN-10: 0-7407-7126-4

This book was conceived, designed,
and produced by iBall, an imprint of
Ivy Press
The Old Candlemakers, West Street,
Lewes, East Sussex, BN7 2NZ, UK

Creative Director Peter Bridgewater
Publisher Jason Hook
Editorial Director Caroline Earle
Senior Project Editor Dominique Page
Art Director Sarah Howerd
Designer Joanna Clinch
Photographers Simon Punter and Andrew Perris
Illustrators Peters & Zebransky

Some of the material contained in this book
was previously published in *The Lost Art
of Towel Origami*, 2005

Printed in China

08 09 10 11 12 10 9 8 7 6 5 4 3 2 1

Acknowledgments

The publishers are grateful to Christy
for supplying the towels used to make
the projects in this book.

www.christy-towels.com

Introduction

TOWEL ORIGAMI is one of the more intriguing arts once practiced by our forebears. Its exact origins are unknown but they have been the subject of much speculation. It has been said that while Queen Cleopatra bathed in milk—which could be for hours at a time—her servants kept her entertained by fashioning cloths into amusing shapes. Another theory has its roots in the frivolous 1920s, when passengers on cruises filled the empty hours in between sipping cocktails by modeling their towels.

Since the real truth is a mystery, you can pick whichever explanation you like the most. What is important to us today is that this unique ancient craft has been rediscovered! Everywhere, happy vacationers are delighted to discover a towel in the shape of an elephant or a swan on their pillow when they return from a day at the beach. (A fun change from the usual chocolate!)

There is clearly a huge difference between creating towel origami and the traditional paper variety. The success or failure of paper origami relies on accuracy and the need for straight, crisp creases in your material—but let's face it, towels just don't respond in the same way as paper. This permits a certain amount of artistic license in this far less disciplined, much more lighthearted form of origami.

Unlike paper origami, the lost art of towel origami leans heavily toward a range of "molding" techniques combined with simple, basic folding methods. All the models featured in this book have been created using these same methods, so you should be able to replicate them easily. Rest assured that the newly rediscovered art of towel origami requires no special skills, equipment, or even patience. Results are achieved in minutes and it's fun to do! A serious sense of humor is all that's required.

Your pack contains two colored magic towels with which to practice. Place them in water for 30 seconds and watch them expand to full-size hand towels. Most of the models in the book can be made using just the magic towels, but as your confidence grows you may choose to use bigger and fluffier towels in the colors of your choice. You don't have to use the towel colors we have chosen—feel free to let your creativity run wild! See the individual instructions for tips and alternatives.

Begin by mastering the basic techniques on the pages that follow, then move on to the individual projects. Each model has been awarded a difficulty rating, and it is recommended that you begin with an "easy" project and tackle a "moderate" or "difficult" one when you feel more confident.

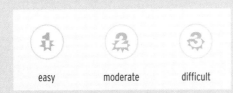

| easy | moderate | difficult |

Whether you choose to fold towels for your own enjoyment or for the entertainment of your family or houseguests, take pleasure in your newfound folding skills. Bath time will never, ever be the same again!

CARING FOR YOUR TOWELS

The towels are made from 100% cotton.

Machine wash cold.
Do not bleach. Iron using medium heat.
Tumble dry on a low heat setting.
Can be dry-cleaned with any solvent
except for trichloroethylene.

7

Basic Folds and Techniques

Due to the soft, fluffy nature of towels, you will understand that the typical crisp folds that are the result of traditional paper origami cannot be re-created exactly. However, most of the very basic traditional folding techniques are employed, alongside more unusual methods, to produce very interesting creations. There is a certain amount of "molding" involved and a fair smattering of slightly more forceful manipulation, too! Here are a few techniques to master before you begin the projects.

Basic Symbols

‑ ‑ ‑ ‑ Dotted lines represent a fold line: either a fold that is made and left creased, or one that is made creased then opened out flat again to indicate the center or a division of the towel's length or width.

↰ This symbol means that you must turn the whole shape over, keeping all previous folds or shaping intact. If necessary, slip one hand under the shape and place the other hand on top, then quickly flip it over.

⟶ Arrows indicate the direction in which the fabric of the towel should be folded, rolled, tucked, or drawn out.

Basic Folds

All the shapes featured in this book begin with a towel that is laid out on a flat surface like the floor or a bed. Make sure that you follow the instructions carefully, and always begin exactly as instructed with the towel laid out horizontally or vertically, as this will affect the final shape of your creation.

Towel Laid Horizontally

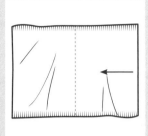

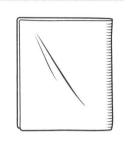

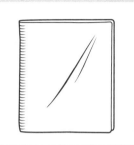

Folding in half widthways

With the towel laid out horizontally, take the farthest right-hand edge

and bring it over to meet the left-hand edge. Now run the palm of your hand along the fold in order

to make a crease. This can be done the opposite way if the instructions direct.

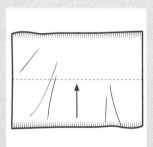

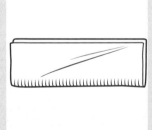

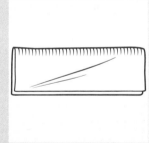

Folding in half lengthways

With the towel laid out horizontally, take the lower edge and bring it

upward to meet the upper edge. Now run the palm of your hand along the fold to make a crease.

This can be done the opposite way if the instructions direct.

Towel Laid Vertically

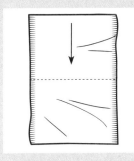
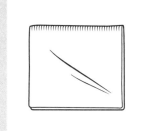

Folding in half widthways
With the towel laid out vertically, take the uppermost edge and bring it down to meet the lower edge.

Now run the palm of your hand along the fold to make a crease.

This can be done the opposite way if the instructions direct.

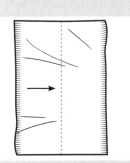
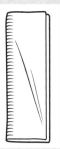

Folding in half lengthways
Take the left-hand edge and bring it over to meet the right-hand edge. Now run the palm of your hand

along the fold to make a crease. This can be done the opposite way if the instructions direct.

NOTE
Use the folding and creasing method to divide the towel into thirds, quarters, or smaller divisions. Fold the towel as required, press the folds to crease, then either use the shape as directed or open up and use the crease lines as markers for further folds.

Rolling and Stretching

Using towels to make models allows for rolling and stretching, whereas traditional origami paper does not. Follow these simple steps to achieve a perfect elephant trunk, a swan neck, or a monkey or pooch body. Some of these techniques take a little while to master, and sometimes a certain amount of force is needed to encourage the model to take the correct shape.

Basic roll

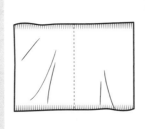

1 Fold and crease the towel to indicate the center line, then open it out flat again.

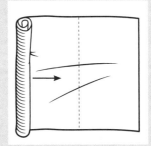

2 Beginning at one short edge, roll the towel tightly toward the center crease line.

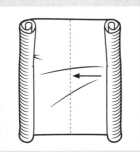

3 Roll up the other half of the towel in the same way, toward the center line.

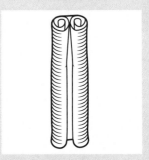

4 The finished shape: two tight rolls lying parallel to each other.

11

Monkey body

This may take a few attempts to get right, and it involves some pulling and heaving!

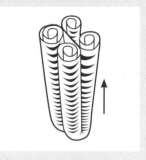

1 Begin with the basic rolled shape (see page 11).

2 Fold the rolled shape in half with the rolls facing upward.

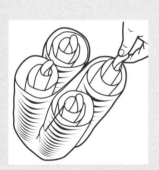

3 Now, this is the difficult part! Pull out the corner of the towel from the center of each roll.

4 Try to hold two corners in one hand and two in the other. Pull the corners away from each other.

5 The folded towel will stretch out to form two legs and two arms. Now manipulate the shape to style it.

Diagonal roll

This fold or roll forms the perfect elephant trunk and swan neck, and is customized a little to form the pooch head (see page 42).

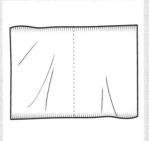

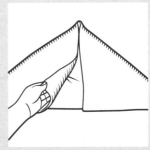

1 Begin with a towel placed horizontally with the center line indicated as shown.

2 Bring the top two corners down to meet the center line, then press the folds flat.

13

3 Roll along each diagonal edge toward the center line.

4 Hold one roll in each hand and twist toward the center tightly. The pointed part will curl into shape.

Pointed Flaps and Tucks

These simple folds result in pointed flaps that can be folded in two directions, and the tuck method allows a right-angled corner to be softened to create a slightly more rounded silhouette. The first method is employed for the angel fish, while the second is useful for molding the ladybug.

Pointed flaps

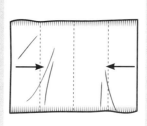

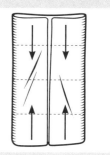

1 Fold a towel in half widthways. Crease the shape into quarters vertically, then open out. Fold right and left sides to meet at the center.

2 Crease the shape to divide it into quarters horizontally, then open out. Bring the top and lower edge to meet in the center.

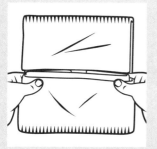

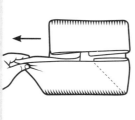

3 Press the shape flat with your palms, then reach inside the lower left-hand side of the shape to find the corner.

4 Pull the corner outward and left into a triangular pointed flap, which can be folded flat. Trace a line with your fingertip as shown by the dotted line.

5 Take the lower right-hand edge and fold it back along the indicated crease line. This makes it easier to bring out the point and fold it downward.

14

Tucks

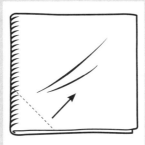

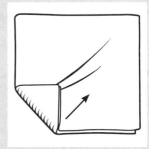

1 Fold a towel in half horizontally, then fold the corner as shown. Press the fold flat with your hand.

2 Keeping your left hand lightly on the folded part, pick up the top layer only of the towel and pull it out from under the folded corner.

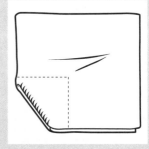

3 Your left hand will now slip inside the shape and the top layer will fall on top.

4 The result is that the corner is now tucked inside the shape to make a more rounded silhouette.

Angel Fish

Inspired by happy memories of sunny holidays in a tropical paradise, these little angel fish can be made from a single color or a combination of pastel or bright colors. As the shape is a simple one, it translates well for towels both large and small, and for face cloths, too. It's a simple task to create a whole shoal of little fishes to swim across the foot of the bed. Not quite the same as being in a tropical paradise, but still lots of fun!

YOU WILL NEED	1 TOWEL 1 FACE CLOTH 1 WIBBLY-WOBBLY EYE OR 1 CHOCOLATE

easy

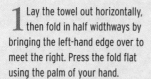 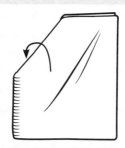 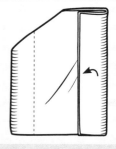

1 Lay the towel out horizontally, then fold in half widthways by bringing the left-hand edge over to meet the right. Press the fold flat using the palm of your hand.

2 Fold the top left-hand corner underneath the shape as shown, then press the fold flat. The diagonal edge should lie approximately at the halfway point along the top and left-hand edges.

3 Fold the shape in half widthways to indicate the center, then open out the shape again. Fold each side inward so they meet at the center crease line. Press the folds flat.

Square face cloths are excellent for making a little entourage of tiny fish to accompany a larger fishy fellow made from a bath towel.

TOP TIP

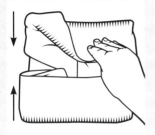

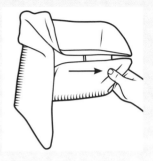

4 Divide the shape roughly into four again but horizontally this time, then fold the top and bottom edges toward the center and press the folds flat.

5 Pull out the left-hand point that lies inside the top fold. When the point is released from the fold, arrange it so it points downward, then press it flat.

6 Repeat with the other point that lies inside the fold on the right-hand side, but this time arrange it so that it points away from the shape. Repeat with the point that lies inside the upper fold as shown.

7 Slip one hand under the shape and lay the other flat on the top. Now flip the shape over to the other side, keeping all the folds in place. The previous points will now resemble fins.

8 Take the face cloth and grasp it in the center. Run the cloth through your hands to form a fin shape. Add it to the tail by tucking it under the fold. Add a chocolate or a wibbly-wobbly eye to finish.

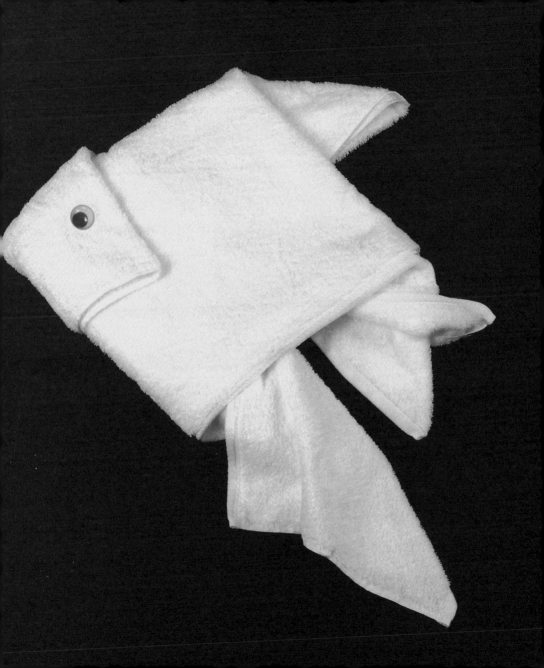

Swan

Seven swans a-swimming? Well, maybe
just one or two would be enough to
make the point! This elegant bird
works perfectly alone, or a pair can
be used to great effect when arranged
symmetrically. You could place some
attractive fragrant soaps or bottles
of bath product on the swan's back
for your guest to enjoy at bath time.

YOU WILL NEED	1 TOWEL 2 FACE CLOTHS (OPTIONAL) SUNGLASSES 2 SAFETY PINS

easy

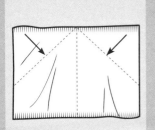

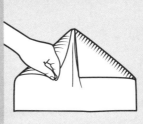

1 Lay out the towel horizontally, then fold in half widthways to indicate the center and press the fold flat. Open up the towel again, then fold the top two corners down to meet at the center.

2 Press the diagonal folds flat using the palm of your hand. Now roll the towel tightly along the diagonal edge at both sides toward the center.

3 When the first side is rolled up tightly, do the same on the other side so the shape is symmetrical. Make sure the first roll does not loosen as you complete the second.

For maximum impact, try using the largest, fluffiest, and most luxurious white towels you can find!

TOP TIP

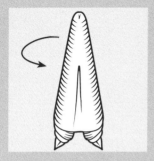

4 Now slip one hand underneath the rolled-up shape and place the other hand on top. Quickly flip the shape over to the other side. This is the swan body.

5 Place your hand on the swan's back and shape the rolled point to form the curved neck. You may have to use a little gentle force to make the neck stay in shape!

6 Locate the edge of the towel that lies across the rolled-up points at the back. Take the edge and roll it back on itself. This action will cause the points to splay outward.

7 Coax the points out a little more and arrange them to form the swan's wings. This will also help the stability of the shape. You can tuck a face cloth into each side to make the wings appear larger.

8 Add a pair of sunglasses to complete this elegant fowl. The weight of the sunglasses also helps to maintain the nicely curved shape of the neck. Use a couple of safety pins to keep the glasses in place.

Turkey

Fan shapes can be used to create a fun Thanksgiving turkey. There are no fancy folding or molding techniques required—it's all just plain, straight, parallel pleats. All you need to do is make sure that the pleats you make are the same width all the way along.

YOU WILL NEED

1 TOWEL AND 1 FACE CLOTH
2 ELASTIC BANDS
2 SAFETY PINS
2 WIBBLY-WOBBLY EYES

easy

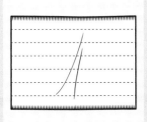

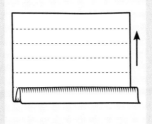

1 Lay the towel out horizontally. Fold and press regular parallel creases across the width about 4 in/10 cm apart. Use your fingers or a warm iron to make really sharp creases.

2 Pleat the towel up along the crease lines now and press flat along the folds with the palm of your hand.

3 Find the center of the pleated shape and secure at this point by winding an elastic band around it. Now fold the shape in half.

If you wash and starch your towels first, the folds of this model will look sharper. You could line the first folded shape with a sheet of tissue paper to help the folds keep their shape.

TOP TIP

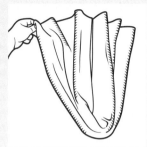

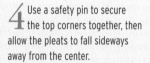

4 Use a safety pin to secure the top corners together, then allow the pleats to fall sideways away from the center.

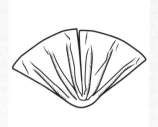

5 Lay the fan shape flat on the bed or prop it up against the pillows at the bed head. Arrange the folds neatly and symmetrically.

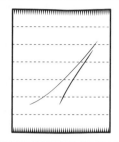

6 Take a face cloth and make small pleats evenly across the whole length as shown. Find the center of the pleated shape as before and bind it with a small elastic band.

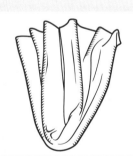

7 Fold the shape in half. Use a safety pin to secure the top edges together as before, then open out the smaller fan shape.

8 When you are satisfied with the fold arrangement of the large fan, place the smaller fan at the base. Ease out and shape your turkey's beak and wattle. Add wibbly-wobbly eyes to finish.

Snail

Snails are really quite beautiful creatures if you look closely, even if they are a bit slimy. It's just a shame they like to eat everything in the garden. This one won't cause any problems, however—no teeth! This model works very well with small towels or even guest-size towels. Try using a striped towel for an eye-catching shell.

easy

1 Lay one towel out horizontally, and indicate a vertical crease down the center. Bring both lower corners to meet the center crease, forming an inverted arrowhead shape. Pat the folds flat.

2 To form the neck, body, and head, roll each diagonal edge tightly toward the center crease line. Secure the folds with two or three safety pins, then flip the shape over.

3 For the shell, lay the second towel out vertically. Bring both side edges to meet at the center. Repeat by bringing both side folds to the center, then hold the towel in half lengthways in order to form a long, thick band.

The snail shell is designed to be thick and soft, so try using two towels together if one appears too small in relation to the head and body shape.

TOP TIP

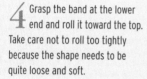

4 Grasp the band at the lower end and roll it toward the top. Take care not to roll too tightly because the shape needs to be quite loose and soft.

5 Use a safety pin to secure the folds at the end of the rolled-up shape. Lay the snail shell on its side and use another two safety pins to secure the end of the roll to the coil underneath, as shown.

6 Lay the body out with the pointed end to the left. This will form the head. The rolled points at the other end will form the tail. Lay the shell on the body, leaving the pointed corners protruding out toward the left-hand side.

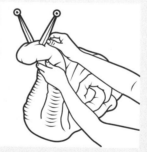

7 Curl the tip of the head and bend the neck backward toward the shell to form a nicely curving shape. To ensure that the head and neck don't uncurl, secure the neck to the shell using a safety pin.

8 Cut out two antennae from the sheet of cardboard. Fold the antennae down the center lengthways and fix in place using tabs of double-sided tape. Add two wibbly-wobbly eyes as shown.

Lobster

Watch out . . . you'll need to be careful when this little chap's about. He's got two very fierce-looking claws, ready to give any unsuspecting bather a little nip! Our lobster forms quite a long but easily manipulated shape. Why not coax the shape to fit around the faucet or at the corner of the bath, then place some pretty shell- or starfish-shaped soaps into his claws to complete the theme.

YOU WILL NEED

2 TOWELS
2 WIBBLY-WOBBLY EYES

easy

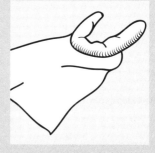

33

1 Lay one towel out vertically and roll up one short edge to approximately one-third the length of the towel.

2 Grasp both ends of the roll and bring them together to form a shallow crescent shape. This will form the lobster's head and claws.

3 Your model should look like this after the first two steps.

You can make a smaller lobster using just one towel. Also try using an elastic band around the body just after step three. It will help to keep the shape together.

TOP TIP

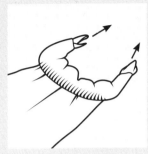

4 You may now begin to manipulate the lobster's snippy claws.

5 Take the other towel and place it on top of the unrolled end of the first, as shown. Now fold the long edges of the second towel around the unrolled section of the first. They should overlap at the center.

6 Now for the body. Make a series of small pleats along the length of the folded towel that lies behind the head and claws. Leave about 4 in/10 cm at the end unpleated.

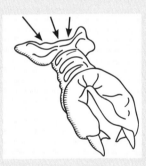

7 Pinch the towel together tightly behind the last pleat, about 4 in/10 cm from the end. Now place your hand inside the folds and spread the towel out to form the fan-shaped tail.

8 Finally, make some minor adjustments to your lobster's head. Stick a pair of wibbly-wobbly eyes to the head to complete the model.

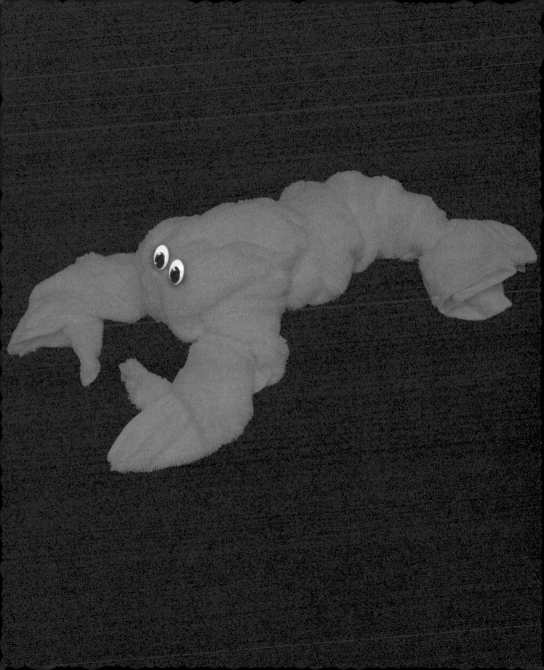

Ladybug

Ladybug, ladybug, fly away home—but
not before I've had a bath, thank you!
This spotted bug requires just a few
basic folding techniques together with
a little "molding" to achieve a nice
plump shape. The fluffy pipe-cleaner
legs aren't absolutely necessary, but
it does make this creature look more
"bug-like," don't you think?

YOU WILL NEED	1 TOWEL 3 FACE CLOTHS BLACK FELT 2 WIBBLY-WOBBLY EYES 6 FLUFFY PIPE CLEANERS

moderate

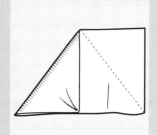 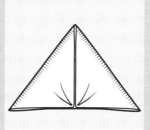 

37

1 Lay the towel out horizontally, fold in half to indicate the center line, then open out again. Bring both top corners down to meet at the center.

2 Press the diagonal folds flat using the palm of your hand. Slip one hand under the shape and lay the other flat on the top. Now flip the shape over, inverting the triangle at the same time.

3 Fold the top two corners downward to meet at the center, and tuck the lower point inside the shape. Press all the folds flat.

Red is the traditional color for a ladybug, but they do come in orange and yellow too, and some are even black with yellow or red spots. Just use your imagination.

TOP TIP

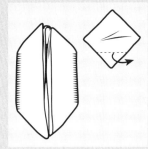

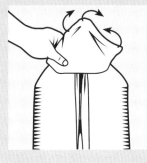

4 Tuck the corners on both sides inside the body shape. This makes a more rounded silhouette. Fold up two face cloths into quarters and tuck inside the wings to give the ladybug a plump body.

5 Take the third face cloth, tuck the lower point underneath, and press the fold flat using the palm of your hand.

6 Place the face cloth onto the top part of the ladybug shape, then tuck the three remaining points behind to form the head.

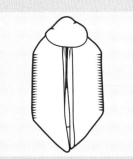

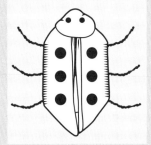

7 Now mold and shape the edges of the ladybug to make a smooth and softly rounded silhouette.

8 Add black felt circles for the spots and a pair of wibbly-wobbly eyes. To make the legs, fold and twist each pipe cleaner around itself.

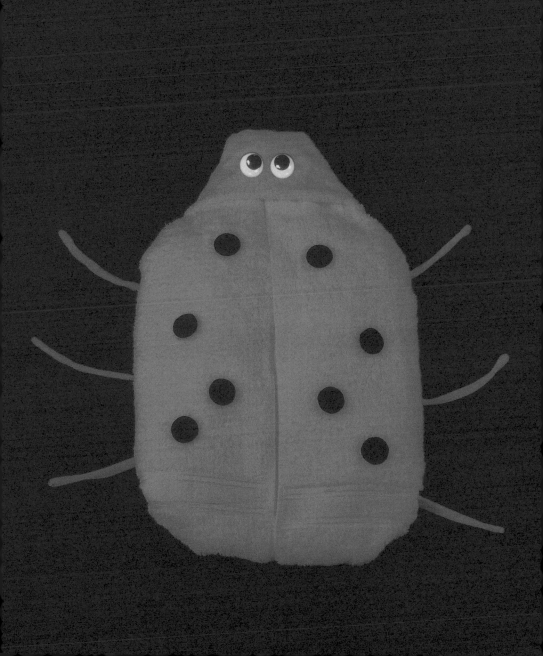

Elephant

What a surprise your guests will have
when they find an elephant on their
bed! For even more impact, try making
a mini herd of jumbos, varying in size
from a tiny one out of face cloths to a
real whopper using large bath towels!
Our elephant looks very smart in lilac,
but for more authenticity use gray.
Alternatively, try a brighter color
such as hot pink or blue.

YOU WILL NEED	2 TOWELS 1 SAFETY PIN SUNGLASSES

moderate

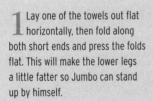 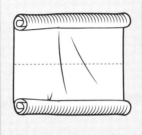 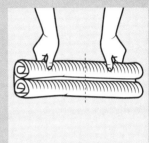

41

1 Lay one of the towels out flat horizontally, then fold along both short ends and press the folds flat. This will make the lower legs a little fatter so Jumbo can stand up by himself.

2 Now fold the towel in half lengthways. Press the fold flat to indicate the center and open out. Now roll the towel up tightly from both long edges so the rolls meet at the crease line in the center.

3 Grasp the rolled-up towel in both hands and bend it in the middle, keeping the rolled side facing outward. Try to make sure that the rolls do not loosen as you do this.

The rolled-up head and trunk shape can sometimes unroll itself.
Secure the shape using a safety pin so that Jumbo won't lose his head while
in situ on your guest's bed or in the bathroom!

 TOP TIP

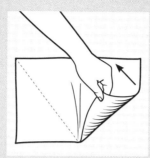 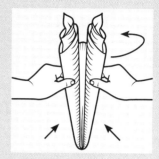

4 Stand the shape up and open out the rolls at the base of each "leg" if necessary so that Jumbo will stand sturdily on a flat surface. You have now completed the elephant body.

5 For the head, lay the second towel out flat, fold in half widthways, and press the fold flat to indicate the center. Open the towel out again, then bring both lower corners to meet the top edge at the center.

6 Roll both diagonal edges toward the center. It is best to do both sides at the same time, if possible. The point at the center will curl slightly, forming the trunk.

7 Turn the shape over and hold the trunk firmly in one hand, then pull down both upper points to form the ears. Open out the towel fabric a little to make a wider ear shape.

8 Place the head onto the body, then add a pair of sunglasses to complete your model.

Pooch

Even the most steadfast non-dog-lover will adore this irresistible little pooch! Anyone, especially children, will love to see this fellow greet them as they walk into their bedroom or bathroom. Based essentially on the elephant shape with just a few slight variations, he's straightforward to make, and the quick addition of the felt features and the wibbly-wobbly eyes piles on the charm.

YOU WILL NEED	2 TOWELS 1 SAFETY PIN BLACK, WHITE, AND RED FELT DOUBLE-SIDED TAPE 2 WIBBLY-WOBBLY EYES

moderate

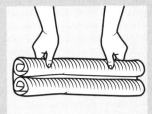

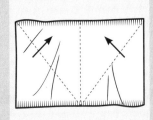

45

1 Lay one towel out horizontally, fold in half to indicate the center, then open out again. Now roll both of the long edges toward the center.

2 Take the rolled shape and bend it to form the dog's body, making sure that the rolls are facing outward. Tuck one end of the shape under so it resembles the back legs in a sitting position.

3 For the head, lay the second towel out, fold in half widthways to indicate the center, then open out again. Now bring the two bottom corners to meet at the center of the top edge, then press the folds flat.

Fido doesn't have to sit up all the time. Simply flatten the rolled-up leg shape so he appears to be lying down, then balance the head on the shape as before.

TOP TIP

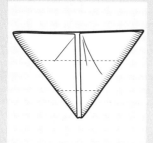

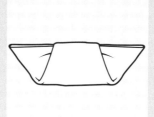

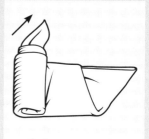

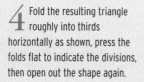

4 Fold the resulting triangle roughly into thirds horizontally as shown, press the folds flat to indicate the divisions, then open out the shape again.

5 Fold the lower point up to meet the second division line, then fold the lower edge to meet the top edge as shown. Press the folded shape flat using the palm of your hand.

6 Take the point at each side and roll up tightly to meet at the center, then pull out the two points a little. At this point secure the rolled shape using a safety pin.

7 Turn the shape over to the other side. Fold the points downward over the dog's face to form the ears. You can roll the edge that lies across the base of the points to release them a little more for shaping.

8 Balance the head on the body, then with double-sided tape apply a felt patch over one eye position; add the wibbly-wobbly eyes, nose, and tongue to complete. Position the features so as to give your pooch the cutest expression!

Polar Bear

Brrr . . . it's chilly up here in the frrrrozen north. Just as well our polar bear has a lovely thick fluffy coat to keep out the cold! He looks like he's out for a casual stroll across the ice, but with a little modification he could adopt a seated pose—simply omit the double fold in step one, then tuck the back legs underneath the body in step two. See "Pooch" on page 44 for an example. If you have a bath towel to spare, why not fold it into a pointed cone shape to resemble an iceberg.

YOU WILL NEED	2 TOWELS 3 SAFETY PINS 2 WIBBLY-WOBBLY EYES

moderate

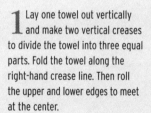

49

1 Lay one towel out vertically and make two vertical creases to divide the towel into three equal parts. Fold the towel along the right-hand crease line. Then roll the upper and lower edges to meet at the center.

2 Bend the rolled-up shape across its center to form the seated shape shown above. The double-thickness rolls will form the polar bear's back legs, and the single-thickness rolls will be the front legs.

3 For the head, lay the other towel out horizontally and bring the side edges to meet at the center. Fold the top two corners toward the center to form a pointed shape. Now pat the fold flat.

You can make a grizzly bear from black or brown towels, or use a combination of black and white to create a panda. For extra cuteness, make two little bear cubs from face cloths or smaller towels.

TOP TIP

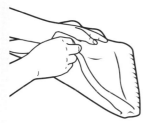

4 Now bring the lower edge upward to line up with the point at the top. Pat all the folds flat. The towel should now be a rectangular shape, laid out horizontally.

5 Make a vertical crease down the center of the rectangle. Take the lower right-hand corner and roll up diagonally to meet the center. Do likewise with the other corner. The result is a squat pointed shape.

6 Pin together securely at the point where the two rolls meet, making sure that the pin cannot be seen.

7 As a result of the first foldings, the two points protrude from the top of the shape. Take each one in turn and form a small, rounded ear.

8 Position the polar bear's head on the seated body shape and hold it in place securely using one or two safety pins. To finish, add two wibbly-wobbly eyes to the head.

Frog

"Ribbit . . . ribbit." Is he a frog or really a handsome prince under an evil spell? You could try kissing him to find out, but I think you might be disappointed. Luckily there are no magical spells here—just some clever rolling and folding and a bit of manipulation to achieve that cheeky "wide-mouthed frog" look. As a thoughtful gesture, why not hide some pretty soaps, chocolates, or a welcome note inside the folds of your frog model, just to surprise a curious guest.

YOU WILL NEED	2 TOWELS 5 SAFETY PINS 2 WIBBLY-WOBBLY EYES

moderate

1 Lay one towel out horizontally, then roll up from the top edge to form a long sausage shape. Secure the overlap at the center with a safety pin so the roll does not come undone. This will form the back legs of the frog.

2 Place one hand on the center of the towel and fashion each side in turn into a frog leg. The shape should resemble an "M" with a flat section at the center. Splay each end of the rolled-up towel to form the frog's webbed feet.

3 Lay the second towel out vertically. Divide it into three equal parts by making vertical creases in the pile. Bring the side edges inward to overlap in the center by folding along the crease lines. Now fold the top two corners inward diagonally to meet at the center.

Our frog looks very nice indeed in plain green, but you can experiment with a spotted towel for the body. If you're feeling particularly artistic, why not give your frog a little silver cardboard crown and turn him into a frog prince!

TOP TIP

4 Roll up the folded towel from the top end to approximately halfway. Secure the roll at each side using two safety pins. This will form the frog's head.

5 Carefully open out the folds of the bottom half of the towel. Then roll up the towel from the edge upward to meet the head shape.

6 Grasp both ends of the rolled-up section and form them around the head to create a crescent shape. These are the frog's arms.

7 Place the head and arms on the flat section at the center of the frog's back legs. You will need to tuck the center of the rolled "arms" under the head to keep them in place.

8 Arrange the head and arms so they balance on the back legs, and secure with safety pins. Manipulate the front of the head to form a big wide mouth. Add two eyes to the tip of the frog's head to complete.

Monkey

This cheeky little guy can be arranged to sit on a bed or chair quite easily (although his head may need a little assistance from a safety pin). Use sunglasses to add character to his face or simply pop on a pair of wibbly-wobbly eyes. The body shape holds together very well due to the nature of the rolls and twists, allowing a little more scope for creative expression. You can hang the monkey by one or both arms from the shower rail in the bathroom, but be sure to use another safety pin to secure his arm so that he stays put!

YOU WILL NEED	2 TOWELS 3 SAFETY PINS 2 WIBBLY-WOBBLY EYES

difficult

57

1 Lay one towel out vertically, fold in half lengthways and press the fold flat to indicate the center, then open out flat again. Roll both the short edges tightly toward the center.

2 Grasp the rolled-up towel in both hands and bend it in the middle. Make sure that the rolls do not loosen as you do so and that the rolls face outward.

3 Find the corner of the towel inside each roll and pull each one out a little. Take two corners in each hand, then pull out firmly in the direction of the arrow. This can be a little difficult at first.

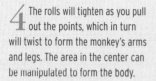

4 The rolls will tighten as you pull out the points, which in turn will twist to form the monkey's arms and legs. The area in the center can be manipulated to form the body.

5 For the head, lay the second towel out flat, then fold in half widthways. Press the fold flat. Now roll the towel diagonally from the top right- and bottom left-hand corners toward the center.

6 Hold the rolls in one hand then roll the bottom point up toward the free points using the other hand. This will form a tight ball shape and the basis of the monkey's head.

7 Turn the rolled shape over and peel the top layer of the point backward to cover the shape and to form the monkey's mouth. Tuck all the ends into the folds behind the head and secure using a safety pin.

8 Arrange the monkey's body so he can sit up or hang from the shower rail, then balance the head on top. Use a safety pin to secure the head to the body. Add wibbly-wobbly eyes to the head to finish.

Pelican

"What a wonderful bird is the pelican, his beak can hold more than his belly can!" That's what Dixon Lanier said, anyway! Our pelican hasn't had his dinner yet, so his beak is looking quite a modest size. Just for fun and authenticity, why not give Mr. Pelican some fish-shaped soaps for his dinner.

YOU WILL NEED	2 TOWELS 2 SAFETY PINS 2 WIBBLY-WOBBLY EYES

difficult

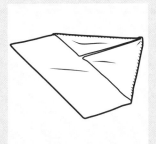

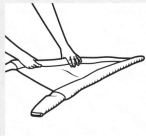

61

1 Lay one towel out vertically and make a horizontal crease along the center line. Bring the top and lower corners on the right-hand side inward to meet the center crease-line, forming an arrowhead shape.

2 Grasp one diagonal fold and roll it up tightly toward the center line. Do likewise with the other fold to form a long, thin pointed shape. The pointed end will form the pelican's head.

3 Flip the shape over, place one hand on the center of the rolls, and bend the pointed end to form an "S" shape. This will become the pelican's head and neck. You may have to coax the towel a little at this stage so it stays in the correct shape.

The pelican is quite an upright shape, so you may have to "persuade" the towels to behave! Try washing and starching them before you begin to give the fabric extra stiffness.

TOP TIP

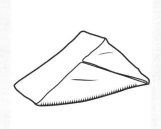

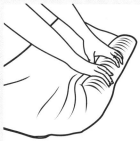

4 Grasp the head and keep it supported throughout the next step. Pinch the towel fabric under the head and gently pull it downward to form the pelican's long beak and large gullet.

5 Lay the second towel out horizontally. Bring the left edge across to meet the right edge. Make a horizontal crease to indicate the center line, then fold the upper and lower right-hand corners down to meet it.

6 Roll up the folded shape from the pointed end toward the center. Stop rolling when you reach the halfway point, then secure the roll using a safety pin at the center.

62

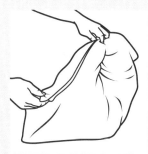

7 Fold the shape in half across the center of the rolled section to form the pelican's wings.

8 Place the pelican's wings onto the body behind the curved neck, then arrange the folds to resemble flapping wings. Add two wibbly-wobbly eyes to the head to complete your model.

Index